FOLLOW IN THE FUTURE WITH THE SHADOW

PROJECT WALZ

Legalizing Marijuana Around the World

GEORGIY SERGEYEVICH GARBUZ

Published 2025

Printed in the United States of America

First Edition
ISBN (softcover): 978-1-963380-72-9
ISBN (hardcover): 978-1-963380-73-6
ISBN (e-book): 978-1-963380-74-3

For information, address:
Holzer Books LLC
8 The Green, Ste. A
Dover, Delaware 19901 USA

For information about special discounts available for bulk purchases, sales promotions, and educational needs, contact:
info@holzerbooksllc.com
+1 (888) 901-7776

holzerbooksLLC®

Contents

CHAPTER 1

A CHOICE FOR THE FUTURE

Life is a series of choices. Some decisions may seem small and inconsequential, while others have the power to shape the trajectory of entire lives, communities, and even nations. Every individual is confronted with the opportunity to pursue different paths—paths of ambition, purpose, or sometimes destruction. The decision to become a doctor, educator, entrepreneur, or even a drug dealer often stems from the opportunities presented—or withheld.

In societies around the world, marginalized communities are frequently burdened by the weight of limited choices. These individuals, particularly underserved youth, face systemic barriers that prevent them from accessing education, healthcare, and economic stability. Yet, even within these constraints, dreams persist—the dream of a better future, a second chance, or a path that leads to opportunity and fulfillment.

This is the fundamental belief that underpins *Project Walz*: that through well-constructed policies and thoughtful legislation, we can provide new and meaningful choices to individuals who have long been denied them. The legalization of non-addictive marijuana is one such choice—a bold, strategic step toward addressing social inequity, boosting economic growth, and reshaping public perception about opportunity and reform.

The Power of Choices in Shaping Lives

The societal impact of individual choices cannot be overstated. A single choice can transform lives, not only for the individual making it but also for families, communities, and future generations. For many who grow up in foster care systems or underserved neighborhoods, the opportunities for upward mobility are scarce. In the absence of resources, they often face two stark realities: become a product of their environment or defy the odds with minimal support.

Georgiy Sergeyevich Garbuz understood this dilemma. His vision for *Project Walz* was born from his desire to replace the limited, often destructive choices available to underserved youth with opportunities for meaningful education, employment, and stability. He believed that by changing the systemic conditions that lead individuals to crime, addiction, or poverty, we can reshape futures and build more equitable societies.

The legalization of marijuana, in this context, is more than a policy shift—it is a platform for empowerment. When structured responsibly, this reform offers a chance to correct historical injustices, provide economic inclusion, and reintegrate individuals from illegal economies into legitimate, thriving industries. By creating new pathways, those who once felt trapped in cycles of limited choices can become active contributors to society, entrepreneurs, and even leaders in their communities.

The Case for Marijuana Legalization

The discussion around legalizing marijuana has long been fraught with controversy. On one side are arguments rooted in fear, fueled by outdated narratives about addiction and moral decay. On the other side is a growing recognition of the economic and social benefits that marijuana reform can bring. Countries and states that have embraced legalization have witnessed reduced crime rates, increased public funding through taxation, and the creation of thousands of jobs.

At its core, marijuana legalization represents a pragmatic response to two interrelated issues: the persistent demand for the product and the failure of prohibitionist policies to curb illegal sales. By bringing cannabis sales into the legal economy, governments can regulate the industry, protect public health, and direct revenues toward social goods like education, healthcare, and public infrastructure.

Project Walz builds upon this premise with a broader, international vision. It not only seeks to legalize non-addictive marijuana within the United States but also establishes a framework for fostering global economic alliances through the International Intergalactic Space Federation (IISF). Revenues generated from legal sales are reinvested into initiatives that transcend national borders, funding space exploration projects, free education for foster care children, and universal healthcare programs.

At its heart, this initiative challenges the narrative that marijuana legalization is simply about profit or convenience. Instead, it positions legalization as a cornerstone of societal progress—a mechanism for fostering economic stability, repairing social divides, and empowering individuals to choose paths of growth rather than survival.

Chapter 2

The Origin of Project Walz

The story of *Project Walz* is rooted in a period of immense uncertainty—the global economic crisis of 2007. Amid the financial collapse that destabilized economies worldwide, a bold vision emerged to not only revive economic growth but also address long-standing social inequities. At the center of this initiative was Georgiy Sergeyevich Garbuz, a leader with an unwavering belief that legalization, when approached with purpose and responsibility, could catalyze meaningful change.

The Economic Crisis of 2007

The financial crisis of 2007 and 2008 marked one of the darkest periods in recent history. Economic downturns in the housing market and financial institutions rippled across the globe, causing massive job losses, foreclosures, and a sense of hopelessness for millions of families. In the United States alone, unemployment soared, and entire communities were left grappling with the harsh realities of economic collapse.

This environment created an urgent need for new economic strategies that could generate revenue, create jobs, and provide relief to struggling sectors of the population. Yet, conventional solutions seemed insufficient to address the scale of the crisis. It was during this turbulent period that an unconventional but ambitious proposal began to take shape: the legalization of non-addictive marijuana as a means to not only stimulate the economy but also reform an outdated system that criminalized millions for non-violent offenses.

The Vision of Georgiy Sergeyevich Garbuz

For Georgiy Sergeyevich Garbuz, this period of economic instability represented both a crisis and an opportunity. His vision for *Project Walz* was deeply personal and grounded in his belief that significant, positive change could be achieved by empowering individuals through education, healthcare, and economic inclusion.

Unlike traditional reform advocates, Garbuz saw marijuana legalization not just as an economic stimulus but as a way to address systemic injustices. His dream extended far beyond the borders of the United States—it encompassed a global initiative that would foster international alliances, fund scientific research, and support space exploration. He envisioned a world where legal cannabis revenues could build **free educational institutions**, especially for foster care children, and provide **universal healthcare** that reached the most vulnerable communities.

His vision was not without its critics, but Garbuz's unrelenting optimism and innovative thinking set the foundation for a movement that would reimagine the very purpose of policy reform. For him, *Project Walz* was not merely about economic gain; it was about creating new possibilities for individuals who had long been denied equitable opportunities.

Initial Conversations and Government Outreach

The path from vision to implementation began with conversations—conversations that would spark both hope and controversy. Garbuz's initial discussions with policymakers, advisors, and advocates focused on presenting marijuana legalization not as a risky social experiment but as a well-planned strategy for economic recovery. One pivotal dialogue involved a man named William, whose support and outreach to government officials played a crucial role in elevating the proposal to national attention.

These early conversations were met with mixed reactions. Some government representatives were wary of the societal backlash that might come from such a bold proposal, especially given the prevailing stigmas surrounding cannabis use. However, others saw the economic and social potential of the initiative, recognizing that a regulated, legal cannabis market could bring substantial revenue and public health improvements while addressing the root causes of illegal trade.

Garnering support required not only addressing economic concerns but also reframing the narrative around legalization. The discussions highlighted that marijuana policy reform was not about promoting drug use but about regulating an existing market, protecting consumers, and reinvesting in public welfare. Garbuz's outreach efforts emphasized that the revenue generated from legalized sales could be channeled into programs that strengthened society as a whole—free education, universal healthcare, and international collaboration on scientific and space-related projects.

A Movement Takes Shape

These initial conversations laid the groundwork for what would become *Project Walz*. What began as an idea born out of economic necessity evolved into a comprehensive strategy for social and economic transformation. The vision of Georgiy Sergeyevich Garbuz remains central to this initiative—a vision that not only responded to the economic devastation of 2007 but also sought to redefine how nations could recover, innovate, and build toward a brighter, more equitable future.

Chapter 3

The Path to Legalization

The journey toward the legalization of non-addictive marijuana has been long and complex, shaped by social and political challenges, deeply ingrained public perceptions, and debates about economic viability. Despite the resistance and stigmas surrounding cannabis, *Project Walz* emerged as a strategic initiative designed to reframe the conversation and present legalization as a tool for social reform, economic growth, and global collaboration.

Social and Political Challenges

The legalization of marijuana has historically been met with significant opposition from both social groups and political institutions. Many policymakers have hesitated to support legalization due to fears of public backlash, concerns about increased substance abuse, and uncertainty about regulation.

Socially, marijuana use has long been associated with negative stereotypes, often reinforced by decades of anti-drug campaigns that framed cannabis as a gateway to criminal behavior and addiction. These narratives disproportionately targeted marginalized communities, resulting in heightened incarceration rates for non-violent offenses and deep mistrust in government institutions tasked with enforcing drug policies.

Politically, the issue of marijuana legalization has been polarizing. Legislators have struggled to balance public safety concerns with the demand for reform. At the federal level, the inconsistencies between state legalization efforts and federal prohibition laws created additional hurdles, leading to jurisdictional conflicts and unclear guidelines for law enforcement and regulatory agencies.

Despite these challenges, proponents of legalization, including Georgiy Sergeyevich Garbuz, recognized that change was possible through clear messaging, strategic partnerships, and comprehensive policies that addressed public concerns. Garbuz believed that legalization required more than legislation—it required a cultural shift in how marijuana was perceived and discussed at both local and global levels.

Public Perception and Stigmas

Public perception has been one of the most significant obstacles in the path to legalization. For decades, cannabis use has been stigmatized as irresponsible, harmful, and inherently criminal. These perceptions were largely shaped by outdated policies and media portrayals that ignored the medicinal, economic, and social potential of the substance.

In many communities, particularly those affected by the war on drugs, cannabis was not only illegal but also a symbol of systemic oppression. This stigma contributed to a cycle of poverty, arrest, and exclusion, making it difficult for individuals with prior convictions to reintegrate into society.

A key objective of *Project Walz* was to challenge these outdated perceptions and emphasize the benefits of regulation over prohibition. The initiative reframed marijuana legalization as a means of protecting consumers through safety standards, generating revenue for public services, and reducing the economic and social burdens associated with incarceration for minor drug offenses. Public education campaigns were integral to this effort, focusing on the science behind non-addictive marijuana, its economic advantages, and its potential to foster innovation in industries such as healthcare, agriculture, and space exploration.

Garbuz understood that public trust was essential for legalization to succeed. By emphasizing transparency, accountability, and community involvement, *Project Walz* aimed to create a sense of shared purpose and demonstrate that legalization was not about promoting drug use but about fostering safer, healthier, and more prosperous communities.

The Economic Potential of Legalization

Amid the social and political challenges, the economic potential of marijuana legalization stood out as an undeniable benefit. The cannabis market, when regulated and taxed, represented a multi-trillion-dollar industry with the capacity to create jobs, reduce government debt, and fund public services such as education and healthcare.

Under *Project Walz*, legalized marijuana sales were projected to generate significant revenue streams that could be reinvested into community development projects. By formalizing the cannabis market and integrating former street-level dealers into legitimate business frameworks, the program not only created opportunities for entrepreneurship but also reduced illegal trade and its associated risks.

The initiative also sought to foster international economic partnerships, inviting allied nations to participate in the regulated market and benefit from shared research, technological advancements, and resource allocation. This global collaboration was designed to strengthen diplomatic ties, support the International Intergalactic Space Federation (IISF), and fund initiatives aimed at space exploration and interplanetary colonization.

By presenting marijuana legalization as a means of economic empowerment, *Project Walz* highlighted its potential to address systemic inequalities, support marginalized communities, and create a sustainable financial foundation for future generations. The initiative positioned legalization not as an end in itself, but as a step toward a more inclusive and innovative global economy.

The path to legalization has been shaped by significant social, political, and cultural hurdles. However, by addressing public concerns, challenging stigmas, and demonstrating the economic benefits of regulation, *Project Walz* has laid the foundation for a policy framework that prioritizes public welfare, economic stability, and international cooperation. Georgiy Sergeyevich Garbuz's vision remains central to this endeavor—a vision that sees legalization not as a divisive issue, but as a unifying force capable of fostering progress and prosperity on a global scale.

CHAPTER 4

THE OWNERSHIP MODEL AND ECONOMIC STRUCTURE

A key pillar of *Project Walz* is its carefully designed ownership model, which balances government oversight with private sector participation. This economic structure is not only meant to regulate the legal marijuana industry but also to foster international collaboration, ensure fair revenue distribution, and support public services such as education and healthcare. The project's ownership framework reflects a commitment to transparency, accountability, and inclusivity, demonstrating how public-private partnerships can serve as engines of both economic progress and social reform.

Public-Private Partnerships Explained

At its core, *Project Walz* operates as a public-private partnership, bringing together government agencies, private corporations, and local entrepreneurs to manage and oversee the legal marijuana industry. This model allows for shared responsibility and benefits. Public entities, such as state and federal governments, play a regulatory role, ensuring that operations comply with laws and that revenues are reinvested into public programs.

Private stakeholders, including corporations and individual investors, bring innovation, efficiency, and capital to the industry.

The public-private partnership approach also ensures that local communities, particularly those previously affected by marijuana-related criminalization, have a stake in the industry's success. By integrating former street-level dealers into legal business frameworks, *Project Walz* aims to formalize informal economies and provide pathways for legitimate employment and entrepreneurship.

This model stands in contrast to purely privatized systems, which can concentrate wealth and exacerbate inequality, and purely state-controlled markets, which may lack the flexibility needed to adapt to consumer demands and industry shifts. Instead, the partnership model represents a balanced approach that combines the strengths of both public oversight and private sector innovation.

International Intergalactic Space Federation (IISF) Involvement

The International Intergalactic Space Federation (IISF) plays a pivotal role in *Project Walz*, not only as a stakeholder but also as a key driver of the project's global vision. The IISF's primary mission is to advance international cooperation in space exploration, and *Project Walz* aligns with this objective by allocating a portion of marijuana-related revenues to support space-related initiatives.

The IISF's involvement adds an international dimension to the project, inviting allied nations to participate in the legal marijuana market as partners rather than competitors. By including IISF member nations in the ownership structure, *Project Walz* fosters economic alliances that strengthen diplomatic ties and promote shared investments in technological research and development. This approach positions marijuana legalization as a tool for both economic growth and international collaboration, with IISF-led initiatives such as space fleet development and planetary colonization benefiting from the project's funding.

Moreover, the IISF's role underscores the potential for economic reforms to transcend national borders and contribute to global progress. By reinvesting legal cannabis revenues into space exploration and scientific discovery, the initiative turns a historically contro-versial industry into a source of innovation and unity.

Ownership Allocations and Stakeholder Roles

The ownership structure of *Project Walz* reflects its commitment to equitable resource distribution and shared prosperity. Each corporation operating under the program is divided into ownership stakes that represent the diverse stakeholders involved.

Forty percent of the corporation's shares are allocated to the state government, ensur-ing that local authorities have a significant stake in the revenue generated within their jurisdiction. Twenty percent is held by the International Intergalactic Space Federation, reinforcing its role as a global partner and beneficiary of the project's success. The federal government holds a ten percent stake, ensuring that national agencies can use the funds to support public programs and infrastructure projects.

Five percent of the ownership is reserved for law enforcement agencies such as the CIA and local police departments. This allocation provides direct funding to public safety initiatives and helps maintain regulatory compliance across the market. Another five percent is designated for international governments allied with the IISF, such as Russia, Ukraine, and Moldova, fostering stronger economic ties between partner nations.

Finally, five percent of the corporation's shares are allocated to local entrepreneurs, in-cluding former street-level dealers who have transitioned into legitimate business owners. This aspect of the ownership model is particularly significant, as it embodies the project's goal of economic reintegration and empowerment. By providing these individuals with legal ownership stakes, the initiative offers them a chance to build wealth, contribute to their communities, and participate in the formal economy.

Each state-level corporation operates a network of retail stores—Minnesota, for example, includes 854 stores across the state. Fifty percent of each store's ownership is reserved for local entrepreneurs, further reinforcing the project's emphasis on localized economic growth. This structure ensures that revenues generated from legal sales directly benefit the communities in which they operate, supporting job creation, entrepreneurship, and public services.

A Model for Inclusive Economic Reform

The ownership model and economic structure of *Project Walz* demonstrate how legalization can be leveraged as a force for social and economic progress. By combining public oversight with private investment and international cooperation, the project creates a framework for sustainable growth and shared prosperity. The initiative's emphasis on equitable resource distribution and stakeholder involvement serves as a blueprint for other industries seeking to balance economic opportunity with social responsibility.

This approach challenges traditional narratives about marijuana legalization, presenting it not as a divisive issue but as a unifying strategy for addressing economic disparities, fostering global alliances, and investing in humanity's collective future.

Chapter 5

Funding Free Education and Healthcare

A cornerstone of *Project Walz* is its commitment to reinvesting marijuana revenues into public programs that enhance societal well-being, with a primary focus on education and healthcare. This initiative underscores the belief that true progress lies not only in economic growth but in ensuring that every individual—particularly those from marginalized backgrounds—has access to the resources necessary to thrive. By directing substantial funds toward free education and universal healthcare, the project aims to build a more equitable and prosperous future for all.

The Vision for Free Space Education

At the heart of the educational initiative is a revolutionary vision: to make high-quality, space-related education accessible to all, regardless of socioeconomic status. Georgiy Sergeyevich Garbuz believed that education should be a universal right rather than a privilege reserved for a select few. His vision encompasses a global network of **Garbuz Space School Academies** dedicated to nurturing the next generation of scientists, engineers, and explorers.

The curriculum at these academies goes beyond traditional STEM education. It includes advanced studies in astrophysics, biotechnology, and environmental sciences, preparing students not only to excel on Earth but also to contribute to humanity's journey into space. By investing in education at this scale, *Project Walz* envisions a future where talented youth—especially those from disadvantaged communities—are empowered to become leaders in the space economy.

In addition to academic excellence, these institutions serve as symbols of hope and opportunity. They stand as proof that reinvestment in public welfare can yield long-term societal benefits, creating a cycle of innovation, progress, and prosperity.

Garbuz Space School Academies: A Legacy for Foster Care Youth

A defining element of the educational program is its focus on foster care children and underserved youth. Georgiy Sergeyevich Garbuz, inspired by his own experiences and observations of societal neglect, envisioned the academies as safe havens where vulnerable children could access world-class education and mentorship.

Foster care children often face significant challenges, including instability, limited educational opportunities, and societal stigma. The Garbuz Space School Academies are designed to address these barriers by providing comprehensive support systems that include free tuition, housing, counseling, and career guidance. By removing financial and social obstacles, the academies offer foster care youth a chance to pursue careers in cutting-edge fields, from space engineering to biomedical research.

This legacy of opportunity reflects the core belief that talent and potential exist in every child, regardless of their circumstances. By investing in foster care children, the program not only uplifts individuals but also strengthens communities and contributes to a more inclusive and resilient society.

Universal Healthcare Initiatives Supported by Marijuana Revenues

In addition to education, *Project Walz* prioritizes healthcare as a fundamental right that should be accessible to all. The revenues generated from legal marijuana sales are earmarked to support universal healthcare programs, ensuring that communities have access to comprehensive medical services.

Healthcare inequalities have long plagued societies, with underserved populations often lacking access to preventive care, mental health support, and life-saving treatments. By directing funds toward universal healthcare, the initiative seeks to close these gaps and promote overall well-being. This includes the establishment of public health clinics, expanded mental health services, and programs focused on preventive care and community wellness.

The healthcare component of *Project Walz* is designed not only to treat illness but also to foster healthier communities through early intervention and education. The program recognizes that healthcare is not a luxury—it is a necessity that underpins economic stability and social cohesion. By ensuring that marijuana revenues are reinvested in public health, the initiative aims to create a system where no one is denied care due to financial constraints.

A Model for Social Investment

The commitment to funding free education and universal healthcare illustrates how economic reform can be leveraged to address systemic inequalities. By prioritizing the needs of foster care youth and underserved populations, *Project Walz* demonstrates that legalization can serve as a vehicle for social progress rather than mere profit. The initiative's focus on reinvestment transforms the cannabis market from a controversial industry into a source of opportunity, equity, and hope.

Ultimately, the educational and healthcare initiatives within *Project Walz* reflect a broader vision of what is possible when public policy prioritizes people over profit. By providing access to world-class education and healthcare, the project lays the foundation for a future where individuals can thrive, communities can flourish, and humanity can work together to achieve extraordinary things—on Earth and beyond.

Chapter 6

Transitioning Illegal Markets

One of the most complex and ambitious aspects of *Project Walz* is its approach to transitioning the illegal marijuana market into a regulated, legitimate industry. While legalization creates significant economic opportunities, it also presents the challenge of addressing entrenched illegal markets that have operated outside the law for decades. To address this issue, *Project Walz* includes a comprehensive strategy aimed at integrating former drug dealers into the legal market while ensuring law enforcement agencies maintain oversight and accountability. This approach not only reduces illegal activity but also creates new avenues for economic inclusion and social reintegration.

The Drug Confession Program Framework

At the heart of this transition strategy is the **Drug Confession Program**—a government-led initiative designed to formalize the participation of former street-level dealers in the legal cannabis economy. This program offers former dealers a structured pathway to legalize their operations by voluntarily confessing their past involvement in illegal activities. In exchange for their cooperation, participants gain access to resources such as business training, legal support, and opportunities to own shares in newly established marijuana corporations.

The program emphasizes transparency and accountability while offering former dealers a chance to start fresh within a legitimate framework. Participants must agree to comply with regulatory requirements and submit to background checks, ensuring that their transition aligns with public safety standards. This initiative demonstrates that legalization is not only about decriminalization but also about fostering rehabilitation and reintegration through economic empowerment.

By acknowledging the realities of illegal markets and providing a structured path to legitimacy, the Drug Confession Program seeks to break cycles of crime and create sustainable alternatives for individuals who were previously excluded from legal economic participation.

Integrating Former Drug Dealers into Legal Markets

One of the primary goals of *Project Walz* is to convert former illegal operators into legitimate business owners and stakeholders within the regulated cannabis market. This approach recognizes that many street-level dealers possess entrepreneurial skills, market knowledge, and networks that can be assets in a legal business setting. Rather than marginalizing these individuals further, the program integrates them into the formal economy, offering them ownership stakes in cannabis corporations and retail stores.

Under the initiative's ownership model, local entrepreneurs—including former dealers—are granted a five percent share in corporations and a fifty percent share in retail stores within their communities. This structure provides former dealers with substantial economic incentives to comply with legal standards and contribute to the success of the industry.

This transition not only improves public safety by reducing illegal trade but also strengthens local economies by creating legitimate job opportunities and fostering community-based entrepreneurship. By shifting former dealers from the shadows into formal roles as legal business partners, *Project Walz* redefines the narrative surrounding rehabilitation and economic inclusion.

Law Enforcement Cooperation and Accountability

A successful transition from an illegal to a legal market requires close collaboration between law enforcement agencies and community stakeholders. To ensure the integrity of the legalization process, *Project Walz* emphasizes cooperation with agencies such as the **police**, **FBI**, and **CIA**. These agencies play a critical role in monitoring compliance, enforcing regulations, and addressing any attempts to circumvent legal requirements.

However, the program also prioritizes **accountability and trust-building** between law enforcement and the communities they serve. Historically, drug enforcement policies have contributed to mistrust and tension, particularly in marginalized communities disproportionately affected by the war on drugs. To address this, *Project Walz* incorporates measures aimed at promoting fairness, transparency, and restorative justice.

Law enforcement agencies participating in the program receive dedicated funding to support their operations, including salaries, training programs, and resources for community engagement initiatives. These funds are intended to shift the focus of law enforcement from punitive measures to supportive oversight, creating a regulatory environment that prioritizes public safety while fostering economic growth.

By fostering collaboration rather than conflict, *Project Walz* seeks to redefine the relationship between law enforcement and former offenders. The program's emphasis on mutual accountability ensures that both law enforcement agencies and entrepreneurs operate within a framework of respect, fairness, and shared responsibility.

A New Era of Economic Inclusion

The transition of illegal markets to legal enterprises is a defining feature of *Project Walz*. By integrating former drug dealers into legitimate roles, the initiative creates pathways for economic empowerment while addressing the root causes of illegal trade. The Drug Confession Program, coupled with strong regulatory oversight and community-based entrepreneurship, demonstrates how legalization can be a catalyst for rehabilitation, social reintegration, and economic transformation.

Through strategic cooperation with law enforcement and comprehensive support for former dealers, *Project Walz* presents a model for creating a more inclusive and accountable cannabis market—one that prioritizes opportunity, safety, and progress for all.

CHAPTER 7
THE INTERNATIONAL SCOPE OF THE PROGRAM

T he economic and social impacts of *Project Walz* extend far beyond national borders, reflecting a commitment to fostering international partnerships and promoting economic growth on a global scale. By inviting allied nations to participate in the legal marijuana market, the program creates opportunities for diplomatic collaboration, resource-sharing, and mutual prosperity. The initiative's global framework emphasizes fair pricing, efficient distribution, and the reinvestment of revenues into public services, making it a model for economic reform that benefits both local and international stakeholders.

Regional Price Comparisons: Kazakhstan, Ukraine, and Russia

One of the defining features of *Project Walz* is its acknowledgment of regional price disparities in the marijuana market. In regions such as **Eccik, Kazakhstan**, **Chernoviche, Ukraine**, and parts of **Russia**, the price of one kilogram of marijuana is estimated to be as low as five dollars. These low regional prices underscore the economic challenges faced by producers and distributors in international markets, where legal and logistical barriers often inflate costs and create supply chain inefficiencies.

By incorporating these regional realities into its economic model, *Project Walz* seeks to create a fair pricing system that benefits both producers and consumers. The program's goal is to stabilize prices by regulating supply, preventing price exploitation, and ensuring that participating nations can compete in the U.S. market without sacrificing profitability. This strategy fosters an equitable marketplace where developing nations can leverage their resources to generate significant revenues while contributing to a shared global economy.

The Container-Based Distribution System

To ensure efficient and transparent distribution, *Project Walz* implements a **container-based system** for transporting and selling legal marijuana. Under this system, each participating city is allocated a specific number of containers based on its population size, demand, and market needs. This approach allows for precise control over supply, minimizing surplus or shortages and ensuring that distribution aligns with consumer demand.

Each corporation involved in the program receives permission to transport and sell containers on a city-by-city basis. Some cities may require larger allocations due to higher demand, while others may require fewer containers. By tailoring distribution to local market conditions, the program optimizes sales and prevents regional imbalances.

In Minnesota, for example, market analysis suggests that the state would require over **44,000 containers** annually to meet consumer demand. This high demand necessitates the establishment of **52 International Intergalactic Space State Drug Corporations** to ensure efficient coverage and service. This container-based approach not only supports economic growth but also serves as a model for how regulated markets can function effectively on a large scale.

Economic Growth at State and Global Levels

The economic benefits of *Project Walz* are designed to extend from individual states to the international community. At the state level, legal marijuana sales are projected to generate substantial revenue streams that can be reinvested into education, healthcare, and public infrastructure. By formalizing the cannabis industry and reintegrating former street-level dealers as legitimate entrepreneurs, the program fosters job creation, entrepreneurship, and community development.

On a global scale, the program invites allied nations to establish **government-part-nered corporations** within the U.S. market, fostering economic interdependence and diplomatic collaboration. These partnerships allow participating nations to benefit from shared research, technological advancements, and revenue streams, strengthening their domestic economies while contributing to a collective international effort.

Moreover, the program's international scope supports the broader objectives of the **International Intergalactic Space Federation (IISF)**. A portion of the revenues generated by *Project Walz* is allocated to IISF-led initiatives, including the development of space exploration projects and planetary colonization efforts. This reinvestment underscores the program's commitment to advancing scientific discovery and creating a future where economic prosperity and technological innovation go hand in hand.

A Global Framework for Progress

By addressing regional price disparities, implementing an efficient distribution system, and fostering international economic collaboration, *Project Walz* establishes a global framework for sustainable growth and shared prosperity. The program's emphasis on fair pricing, resource-sharing, and international partnerships demonstrates how economic reform can transcend national borders and contribute to a more interconnected and inclusive world.

Through its international scope, *Project Walz* not only strengthens domestic markets but also reinforces global alliances, positioning legalization as a means of fostering unity, progress, and innovation on a planetary scale.

Chapter 8

Minnesota as a Case Study

To understand the real-world implications of *Project Walz*, Minnesota serves as an ideal case study. The state's projected demand for legal marijuana, its regulatory framework, and its economic potential illustrate how the initiative can operate at a state level while contributing to broader national and international goals. By examining Minnesota's market needs and expected revenues, we gain insight into how the program's innovative distribution and ownership model can drive local economic growth, foster job creation, and reinvest profits into public welfare programs.

Walz International Space Drug State Corporation of Minnesota

The **Walz International Space Drug State Corporation of Minnesota** is a prototype designed to demonstrate how the legal cannabis market can function under the public-private partnership model proposed by *Project Walz*. This corporation operates as a joint venture involving state government agencies, private sector stakeholders, and local entrepreneurs, with oversight and funding support from the federal government and the International Intergalactic Space Federation (IISF).

The Minnesota corporation adheres to the ownership structure established by the program, with 40% of the stake held by the state government, 20% by the IISF, and smaller shares allocated to federal agencies, law enforcement, and international partners. Crucially, 5% of the ownership is reserved for local entrepreneurs, including former street-level dealers who have transitioned into legitimate business roles.

This organizational structure not only ensures that revenues are distributed equitably but also fosters accountability and transparency. By granting local stakeholders a meaningful share of ownership, the corporation reinforces the program's commitment to economic inclusion and empowerment.

Market Demand and Container Projections

Market analysis conducted in Minnesota reveals a high demand for legal marijuana, reflecting the growing consumer base and the potential for substantial economic returns. According to program projections, the state would require approximately **44,408 containers** of legal marijuana annually to meet market demand. This figure highlights the significant volume of product needed to sustain the legal market and underscores the importance of an efficient distribution system.

To accommodate this demand, Minnesota is set to establish **52 International Intergalactic Space State Drug Corporations** across the state, each responsible for managing the transportation, storage, and sale of containers within their designated regions. These corporations will oversee a network of retail outlets, ensuring that consumers in both urban and rural areas have access to regulated, safe products.

The container-based system allows for precise control over supply, minimizing the risk of shortages or surpluses. By tailoring distribution to market conditions, the program optimizes sales and maximizes revenue generation, creating a model for scalability and adaptability across other states and regions.

Revenue Impact on Local Communities

The revenues generated by legal marijuana sales in Minnesota are expected to have a transformative impact on local communities. With each container estimated to contribute millions of dollars in sales, the total revenue generated by the state's legal market will fund critical public services, including education, healthcare, and infrastructure projects.

One of the primary beneficiaries of this revenue is the state's educational system. Funds will be directed toward the establishment and operation of **Garbuz Space School Academies**, which provide free, high-quality STEM education to foster care children and underserved youth. By investing in education, the program not only addresses social inequities but also prepares the next generation for careers in the space economy and other high-demand fields.

Healthcare initiatives will also receive substantial funding, supporting the expansion of mental health services, preventive care programs, and community health clinics. By reinvesting marijuana revenues into public health, the program seeks to reduce health disparities and improve overall well-being across the state.

Moreover, the program's economic model creates thousands of jobs, from cultivation and distribution roles to retail and regulatory positions. This job creation fosters economic stability and reduces unemployment, particularly in communities that have historically been marginalized by drug enforcement policies.

By integrating former illegal operators into the legal market as business partners and employees, the initiative also promotes social reintegration and economic mobility. The program's emphasis on local ownership and entrepreneurship ensures that the economic benefits of legalization remain within the communities most affected by past criminalization.

A Blueprint for National Implementation

Minnesota's experience with *Project Walz* serves as a blueprint for other states seeking to implement similar programs. The state's high market demand, strategic distribution network, and commitment to reinvestment demonstrate how legalization can be managed effectively to maximize economic returns and support public welfare.

Through its ownership model, container-based system, and focus on community development, the program illustrates how the transition from an illegal to a legal market can create sustainable economic growth while fostering trust, accountability, and equity.

By examining Minnesota as a case study, we see how *Project Walz* can turn legalization into a catalyst for transformative change, not only at the state level but also as part of a national and global movement toward economic inclusion and social progress.

Walz International Space Drug State Corporation of Minnesota

T he **Walz International Space State Drug Corporation** is a bold and transformative initiative designed to stimulate local, national, and global economies while advancing humanity's exploration of space. Rooted in the principles of *Project Walz*, this program underscores the potential of legalizing non-addictive marijuana to support economic revitalization, social reintegration, and scientific progress.

With the endorsement of policymakers and global partners, the initiative played a pivotal role in legalizing marijuana in the United States and now aims to advocate for its global legalization. By creating regulated markets that replace illegal sales, the program establishes sustainable economic frameworks that uplift communities and generate significant public revenue.

Strategic Economic Partnerships and Production Goals

The program is strategically designed to partner with nations experiencing economic challenges, creating opportunities for marijuana cultivation that benefit both local producers and international markets. Drawing from historical data, such as 2003 prices in **Esik (Kazakhstan)**, **Novaia Sinjereia (Moldova)**, and **Chernovchi (Ukraine)**, where marijuana was valued between $5–$10 per kilogram, the initiative highlights the disparity between production costs and the $3,000 per kilogram price in the U.S. black market. This discrepancy underscores the immense potential for profit within a regulated, legal framework.

By purchasing and cultivating marijuana in these regions, *Project Walz* not only provides economic relief to struggling communities but also redirects profits away from illegal markets and into public programs.

Projected Sales and State Operations

Research indicates that one container, weighing **40,000 pounds**, can be sold within a week, with projected annual profits reaching **$200 million** per container across multiple regions. In Minnesota alone, fulfilling the state's demand would require **52 International Space Drug State Corporations**, collectively generating **$147.96 trillion** in annual sales revenue.

The program ensures that each state maintains regulatory control over its marijuana market by establishing state-run corporations that oversee distribution, transportation, and sales. These state corporations collaborate with local entrepreneurs, allowing communities to participate in the market through partner-owned stores in every city. This framework ensures that economic gains remain within the state while contributing to federal and international initiatives.

To meet the nationwide demand, the program projects the need for **2.37 million containers annually** across all states, each regulated to support public welfare initiatives, such as free education and healthcare.

Transitioning from Illegal to Legal Markets

A critical component of the initiative is its **Former Dealer Integration Program**, which facilitates the reintegration of former street-level dealers into legal enterprises. By providing business training, legal support, and access to ownership opportunities, the program empowers individuals to transition into legitimate roles within the cannabis market.

This approach ensures that economic participation is accessible to individuals who were previously marginalized, fostering rehabilitation and reducing illegal trade. However, the success of this transition relies on public support and trust, reinforced by transparent policies, community outreach, and regulatory oversight.

Ownership Structure of Walz International Space Drug State Corporations

Each **Walz International Space Drug State Corporation** is structured to balance public oversight with private-sector collaboration, ensuring that economic benefits are equitably distributed among stakeholders. The ownership allocations are as follows:

- **40%**: State Government (for reinvestment in public services, education, and healthcare)

- **20%**: International Intergalactic Space Federation (IISF) to support space exploration and planetary colonization

- **10%**: Federal Government (for national public programs and infrastructure)

- **10%**: NASA (for research and technological development)

- **5%**: Law Enforcement (CIA, Interpol, FBI, or military agencies for regulatory oversight)

- **5%**: State or Federal Police (to maintain local law enforcement presence and ensure compliance)

- **5%**: International Government Partners (e.g., Russia, Moldova, Mexico, reinforcing diplomatic ties)

- **5%**: Local Business Owners, Entrepreneurs, or Former Dealers (contingent on meeting government criteria and passing regulatory reviews)

This ownership model reflects the program's commitment to economic inclusivity, transparency, and international cooperation. By including local business leaders and former dealers as stakeholders, the initiative fosters community empowerment and social reintegration.

A Future of Economic Prosperity and Space Exploration

The **Walz International Space Drug State Corporation** initiative envisions a future where regulated markets drive economic growth, fund public services, and support humanity's next great leap into space. By leveraging the revenues generated through legalization, the program aligns economic policy with global scientific ambitions, funding space-related projects such as spacecraft development and planetary research led by the IISF.

This initiative demonstrates that legalization, when managed through a structured and inclusive framework, can be a force for unity, progress, and exploration. By integrating economic reform with public welfare and scientific discovery, *Project Walz* paves the way for a world where nations prosper together and humanity expands its horizons beyond Earth.

City-Level Implementation in Minnesota

The success of the *Walz International Space Drug State Corporation of Minnesota* depends on its ability to create a localized network of partner corporations in cities across the state. This strategy ensures that the economic benefits of legalization reach even the smallest communities, creating employment opportunities, fostering local entrepreneurship, and strengthening public infrastructure. By distributing ownership stakes to local business leaders and former street-level dealers, the initiative reinforces its commitment to economic inclusion, rehabilitation, and social progress.

Each **Walz International Space Drug State Corporation** follows the same ownership structure to balance public oversight with community engagement and local entrepreneurship:

- 40%: Walz International Space Drug State Corporation of Minnesota (Owner)

- 10%: International Intergalactical Space Federation

- 50%: Local Businessmen or Former Drug Dealer (subject to meeting all government agency requirements)

This model allows for both central regulation and local empowerment, creating a seamless system of accountability and economic reinvestment.

Current and Planned City-Level Corporations

The following cities have established or planned **Walz International Space Drug State Corporations** operating under the same ownership model:

Ada, Adams, Adrian, Afton, Aitkin, Akeley, Albany, Albert Lea, Albertville, Alden, Alexandria, Aitura, Alvarado, Amboy, Andover, Annandale, Anoka, Appleton, Argyle, Arlington, Ashby, Askov, Atwater, Audubon, Aurora, Austin, Avon, Babbitt, Backus, Badger, Bagley, Balaton, Barnesville, Barnum, Barrett, Battle Lake, Baudette, Baxter, Bayport, Beardlsey, Beaver Creek, Becker, Belgrade, Belle Plaine, Bellingham, Belview, Bemidji, Benson, Bertha, Bethel, Big Falls, Big Lake, Bigelow, Bigfork, Bird Island, Biwabik, Blackduck, Blooming Prairie, Blue Earth, Bluffton, Bovey, Bowlus, Boyd, Braham, Brainerd, Brandon, Breckenridge, Brewster, Bricelyn, Brooten, Browerville, Browns Valley, Brownsdale, Brownsville, Brownton, Buckman, Buffalo Lake, Buffalo, Buhl, Burnsville, Butterfield, Byron, Caledonia, Calumet, Cambridge, Campbell, Canby, Cannon Falls, Canton, Carlos, Carlton, Carver, Cass Lake, Center City, Ceylon, Champlin, Chandler, Chanhassen, Chaska, Chatfield, Chisago City, Chisholm, Chokio, Circle Pines, Clara City, Claremont, Clarissa, Clarkfield, Clarks Grove, Clear Lake, Clearbrook, Clearwater, Cleveland, Climax, Clinton, Cloquet, Cohasset, Cokato, Cold Spring, Coleraine, Cologne, Comfrey, Cook, Cosmos, Cottage Grove, Cottonwood, Courtland, Crookston, Crosby, Crosslake, Crystal Bay, Currie, Cyrus, Dakota, Dalton, Danube, Darwin,

Dassel, Dawson, Dayton, Deer Creek, Deer River, Deerwood, Delano, Delavan, Detroit Lakes, Dexter, Dilworth, Dodge Center, Donnelly, Dover, Duluth, Dundas, Eagle Bend, Eagle Lake, East Grand Forks, Easton, Echo, Eden Prairie, Eden Valley, Edgerton, Eitzen, Elbow Lake, Elgin, Elk River, Elko, Ellendale, Ellsworth, Elmore, Ely, Elysian, Emily, Emmons, Erskine, Evansville, Eveleth, Excelsior, Eyota, Fairfax, Fairmont, Faribault, Farmington, Felton, Fergus Falls, Fertile, Fifty Lakes, Finlayson, Fisher, Flensburg, Floodwood, Foley, Forest Lake, Foreston, Fosston, Fountain, Franklin, Frazee, Freeborn, Freeport, Frost, Fulda, Garfield, Garrison, Gary, Gaylor, Geneva, Ghent, Gibbon, Gilbert, Gilman, Glencoe, Glenville, Glenwood, Glyndon, Gonvick, Good Thunder, Goodhue, Graceville, Granada, Grand Marais, Grand Meadow, Grand Rapids, Granite Falls, Green Isle, Greenbush, Greenwald, Grey Eagle, Grove City, Grygla, Hackensack, Hallock, Halstad, Hamburg, Hampton, Hancock, Hanley Falls, Hanover, Hanska, Hardwick, Harmony, Harris, Hartland, Hastings, Hawley, Hayfield, Hayward, Hector, Henderson, Hendricks, Hendrum, Henning, Herman, Heron Lake, Hewitt, Hibbing, Hill City, Hills, Hinckley, Hitterdal, Hoffman, Hokah, Holdingford, Holland, Hollandale, Hopkins, Houston, Howard Lake, Hoyt Lakes, Hugo, Hutchinson, International Falls, Inver Grove Heights, Ironton, Isanti, Isle, Ivanhoe, Jackson, Janesville, Jasper, Jeffers, Jenkins, Jordan, Kandiyohi, Karlstad, Kasota, Kasson, Keewatin, Kelliher, Kellogg, Kennedy, Kensington, Kenyon, Kerkhoven, Kiester, Kimball, La Crescent, Lafayette, Lake Benton, Lake Bronson, Lake City, Lake Crystal, Lake Elmo, Lake Lillian, Lake Park, Lake Wilson, Lakefield, Lakeland, Lakeville, Lamberton, Lancaster, Lanesboro, Le Center, Le Roy, Le Sueur, Leota, Lester Prairie, Lewiston, Lewisville, Lindstrom, Lismore, Litchfield, Little Falls, Littlefork, Long Lake, Long Prairie, Lonsdale, Loretto, Lowry, Lucan, Luverne, Lyle, Lynd, Mabel, Madelia, Madison Lake, Madison, Magnolia, Mahnomen, Mankato, Mantorville, Maple Lake, Maple Plain, Mapleton, Marble, Marine On Saint Croix, Marshall, Mayer, Maynard, Mazeppa, Mcgregor, Mcintosh, Medford, Melrose, Menahga, Mendota, Middle River, Milaca, Milan, Milroy, Miltona, Minneapolis, Minneota, Minnesota City, Minnesota Lake, Minnetonka Beach, Minnetonka, Montevideo, Montgomery, Monticello, Montrose, Moorhead, Moose Lake, Mora, Morgan, Morris, Morristown, Morton, Motley, Mound, Mountain Iron, Mountain Lake, Murdock, Nashwauk, Naytahwaush, Nerstrand, Nevis, New Auburn, New Germany, New London, New Market, New Munich, New Prague, New Richland, New Ulm, New York Mills, Newfolden, Newport, Nicollet, Nisswa, North Branch, Northfield, Northome,

Northrop, Norwood, Oak Park, Ogilvie, Oklee, Olivia, Onamia, Oronoco, Orr, Ortonville, Osakis, Oslo, Osseo, Ostrander, Ottertail, Owatonna, Park Rapids, Parkers Prairie, Paynesville, Pelican Rapids, Pemberton, Pennock, Pequot Lakes, Perham, Peterson, Pierz, Pillager, Pine City, Pine Island, Pine River, Pipestone, Plainview, Plato, Plummer, Ponemah, Preston, Princeton, Prinsburg, Prior Lake, Racine, Randall, Randolph, Raymond, Red Lake Falls, Red Wing, Redby, Redlake, Redwood Falls, Remer, Renville, Rice, Richmond, Rochester, Rock Creek, Rockford, Rockville, Rogers, Rollingstone, Rose Creek, Roseau, Rosemount, Rothsay, Round Lake, Royalton, Rush City, Rushford, Rushmore, Russell, Ruthton, Sabin, Sacred Heart, Saint Bonifacius, Saint Charles, Saint Clair, Saint Cloud, Saint Francis, Saint Hilaire, Saint James, Saint Joseph, Saint Martin, Saint Michael, Saint Paul Park, Saint Paul, Saint Peter, Saint Stephen, Sanborn, Sandstone, Sartell, Sauk Centre, Sauk Rapids, Savage, Sebeka, Shafer, Shakopee, Shelly, Sherburn, Silver Bay, Silver Lake, Slayton, Sleepy Eye, South Haven, South Saint Paul, Spicer, Spring Grove, Spring Lake, Spring Park, Spring Valley, Springfield, Stacy, Staples, Starbuck, Stephen, Stewart, Stewartville, Stillwater, Stockton, Storden, Sturgeon Lake, Swanville, Taconite, Taunton, Taylors Falls, Thief River Falls, Tower, Tracy, Trimont, Truman, Twin Valley, Two Harbors, Tyler, Ulen, Underwood, Upsala, Utica, Vergas, Vermillion, Verndale, Vernon Center, Vesta, Victoria, Villard, Virginia, Wabasha, Wabasso, Waconia, Wadena, Wahkon, Waite Park, Waldorf, Walker, Walnut Grove, Wanamingo, Warren, Warroad, Waseca, Watertown, Waterville, Watkins, Watson, Waubun, Waverly, Wayzata, Welcome, Wells, West Concord, Westbrook, Wheaton, White Earth, Willernie, Williams, Willmar, Willow River, Wilmont, Windom, Winger, Winnebago, Winona, Winsted, Winthrop, Wood Lake, Worthington, Wrenshall, Wykoff, Wyoming, Zimmerman, Zumbrota.

Economic Impact and Projections

There are a total of **912 cities** in Minnesota. By selling containers to each city through this corporation, the projected annual sales revenue amounts to **$54,720,000,000**. To meet the demand of the Minnesota market, **52 International Space State Corporations** are required to ensure comprehensive coverage and maximize economic benefits.

This expansive network reflects the initiative's commitment to generating wealth at the local, state, and national levels, reinforcing Minnesota's role as a leader in public reinvestment and community development.

Chapter 9

Addressing Illegal Trade and Ensuring Compliance

O ne of the primary challenges faced by marijuana legalization initiatives is the persistence of illegal markets that continue to operate outside of regulatory frameworks. Despite the promise of economic growth and public welfare improvements, the illegal trade often undercuts legal sales, perpetuating unregulated activity that poses public safety risks. *Project Walz* directly addresses this issue by integrating street-level dealers into the legal system, implementing robust public safety measures, and ensuring that tax revenues are reinvested in community programs that promote social and economic stability.

The Role of Street-Level Dealers in Legalization

A unique aspect of *Project Walz* is its recognition that street-level dealers have long played a significant role in the cannabis market and possess valuable insights into consumer needs, distribution networks, and local demand. Rather than excluding these individuals from the legal industry, the program seeks to transition them into legitimate business roles as stakeholders, store owners, and entrepreneurs.

By granting local entrepreneurs—many of whom are former street-level dealers—a five percent ownership stake in legal marijuana corporations and fifty percent ownership of individual retail stores, *Project Walz* provides an economic incentive for these individuals to abandon illegal activities. This ownership model empowers former dealers to build legitimate businesses, generate income, and contribute to their communities.

This approach not only reduces the size of the illegal market but also helps to rebuild trust in the legal system, as former offenders become active participants in regulatory compliance rather than adversaries of the law. The integration of former dealers into the formal economy represents a significant step toward fostering social reintegration and economic inclusion.

Strategies for Public Safety and Market Transparency

Ensuring public safety and maintaining market transparency are key priorities for *Project Walz*. The program includes several strategies designed to prevent illegal activity, monitor compliance, and protect consumers.

First, the program implements advanced tracking and verification systems for every container of legal marijuana, ensuring that products can be traced from cultivation to retail sale. This system prevents illegal diversion of products and assures consumers that the cannabis they purchase is safe, regulated, and free from harmful additives.

Second, comprehensive licensing and training programs are required for all participants in the legal market, from cultivators and distributors to retail employees. These programs ensure that all stakeholders understand regulatory requirements and follow established safety protocols.

Third, the program promotes community engagement and education, providing the public with information about the benefits of legalization, the risks associated with unregulated products, and the role of law enforcement in maintaining a safe and transparent market. By fostering public awareness, the initiative builds trust in the legal market and encourages consumers to choose regulated products over illegal alternatives.

Additionally, *Project Walz* prioritizes collaboration with law enforcement agencies such as the police, FBI, and CIA to monitor market activity and address potential violations. However, the program emphasizes that law enforcement's role should be supportive rather than punitive, focusing on fostering compliance rather than perpetuating criminalization.

Impact of Tax Revenues on Community Programs

One of the most significant benefits of legal marijuana sales is the substantial tax revenue generated, which is reinvested into community programs aimed at improving public welfare. Under *Project Walz*, a portion of these revenues is allocated to support education, healthcare, and public infrastructure projects.

Education programs, particularly the **Garbuz Space School Academies**, receive funding to provide free, high-quality STEM education to foster care children and underserved youth. This reinvestment helps address educational disparities and prepares students for leadership roles in the emerging space economy.

Healthcare initiatives also benefit from marijuana tax revenues, supporting the expansion of mental health services, preventive care programs, and community health clinics. These programs aim to improve access to medical care for marginalized populations and reduce health disparities across communities.

Additionally, public infrastructure projects funded by marijuana revenues include the construction of schools, community centers, and transportation systems. These investments contribute to the overall quality of life by creating safe, vibrant public spaces and improving connectivity within and between communities.

By directing tax revenues toward programs that address systemic inequalities, *Project Walz* demonstrates how legalization can be leveraged to foster social progress and economic empowerment. The program's emphasis on community reinvestment ensures that the benefits of legalization extend beyond individual stakeholders to support the collective well-being of society.

A Comprehensive Approach to Reform

By addressing illegal trade, promoting public safety, and reinvesting revenues into community programs, *Project Walz* presents a comprehensive approach to marijuana legalization. The program's emphasis on economic inclusion, regulatory compliance, and community engagement ensures that the transition from an illegal to a legal market is both effective and equitable.

Through strategic partnerships, transparency measures, and social reinvestment, *Project Walz* aims to build a legal cannabis market that not only generates economic growth but also strengthens public trust, fosters social cohesion, and supports the long-term development of communities.

CHAPTER 10

BUILDING AN INTERNATIONAL ALLIANCE

The success of *Project Walz* extends beyond national borders, as its framework is designed to foster international collaboration and shared prosperity. By inviting allied nations to participate in the legal marijuana market and reinvesting revenues into global initiatives, the project establishes economic partnerships that strengthen diplomatic ties and advance humanity's collective ambitions. At the heart of this international alliance is a shared vision of economic stability, technological innovation, and interplanetary exploration.

The Economic Benefits for Allied Nations

One of the primary objectives of *Project Walz* is to create economic opportunities for partner nations by integrating them into the U.S. legal marijuana market. Countries allied through the International Intergalactic Space Federation (IISF) are granted the ability to establish government-partnered corporations with ownership stakes in the cannabis industry. This provides participating nations with a valuable revenue stream, allowing them to bolster their domestic economies and invest in essential public services.

By entering the regulated U.S. market, allied nations can benefit from increased trade, foreign investment, and the exchange of expertise. The program's ownership model also ensures that profits are distributed equitably, with a portion of the earnings reinvested in scientific research, education, and space exploration projects. This collaborative economic approach strengthens the financial independence of partner nations, empowering them to pursue their developmental goals while contributing to a shared global economy.

Furthermore, the inclusion of international stakeholders fosters economic resilience by diversifying revenue sources. In an increasingly interconnected world, this economic diversification helps mitigate risks and creates a foundation for sustained growth and prosperity across multiple regions.

Strengthening Diplomatic Relations Through Economic Partnerships

Project Walz represents more than an economic initiative—it is a diplomatic strategy aimed at reinforcing alliances and promoting global cooperation. By offering allied nations the opportunity to participate in a transparent, regulated market, the project positions economic collaboration as a tool for strengthening international partnerships.

Economic interdependence creates a mutual incentive for stability, trust, and continued collaboration. Countries that participate in the program gain not only financial rewards but also a stake in the long-term success of broader international initiatives, such as space exploration and scientific innovation. This shared investment fosters a sense of unity and shared purpose, reinforcing diplomatic ties and promoting peaceful relations.

Additionally, the program's inclusive framework ensures that smaller or economically disadvantaged nations can also benefit from the initiative. By providing access to ownership opportunities and revenue streams, *Project Walz* supports economic equity among IISF member nations, reinforcing the principle that progress in one country can contribute to the prosperity of all.

Space Exploration as a Shared Global Priority

One of the defining features of *Project Walz* is its commitment to using marijuana revenues to support space exploration initiatives led by the International Intergalactic Space Federation (IISF). These revenues fund critical projects such as spacecraft development, planetary colonization efforts, and advanced research into interstellar travel. By reinvesting in space exploration, the program aligns economic reform with humanity's long-standing ambition to expand its presence beyond Earth.

The IISF's involvement in *Project Walz* ensures that space exploration remains a collective endeavor rather than an exclusive pursuit by a few nations. By fostering international collaboration, the program positions space exploration as a unifying goal that transcends political and cultural boundaries. Participating nations contribute resources, research, and expertise, making interplanetary exploration a truly global achievement.

Furthermore, the technological advancements driven by space exploration projects have practical applications that benefit life on Earth. Innovations in energy, transportation, and medicine, often developed in pursuit of space travel, have the potential to revolutionize industries and improve everyday living conditions. By investing in these projects, *Project Walz* not only fuels humanity's cosmic aspirations but also drives scientific discovery that enhances global development.

A Framework for Global Unity and Progress

Project Walz demonstrates how economic partnerships can be leveraged to strengthen diplomatic relations, foster international cooperation, and achieve shared goals such as space exploration. By creating a framework that supports economic growth, technological innovation, and global collaboration, the initiative positions legalization as a catalyst for unity and progress.

Through its emphasis on economic inclusion, transparent partnerships, and reinvestment in scientific advancements, *Project Walz* illustrates how legalization can contribute to a future defined by shared prosperity, exploration, and discovery. The program's international alliance model reinforces the belief that humanity's greatest achievements are possible when nations work together toward a common vision.

Chapter 11

Project Lyubov: A Bridge for Peace

At its core, *Project Walz* is not only an economic and social reform initiative but also a blueprint for fostering international peace and stability. A significant component of this vision is *Project Lyubov*, a peace-building initiative designed to address the conflict between Russia and Ukraine by emphasizing economic collaboration and mutual prosperity. By aligning legalization policies with peacebuilding efforts, *Project Lyubov* demonstrates how economic interdependence and shared investments can serve as powerful tools for conflict resolution and long-term cooperation.

The Russian-Ukraine Peace Treaty and Economic Collaboration

The conflict between Russia and Ukraine has been one of the most significant geopolitical crises of the 21st century, causing widespread devastation and straining international relations. *Project Lyubov* emerged as a strategic effort to bridge the divide by promoting economic collaboration as a means of rebuilding trust and fostering peaceful relations.

Central to this initiative is the creation of joint economic opportunities within the framework of the **International Intergalactic Space Federation (IISF)**. By participating in the legal marijuana market through government-partnered corporations, both Russia and Ukraine gain access to significant revenue streams that can be reinvested in rebuilding infrastructure, supporting public services, and strengthening their domestic economies. This economic collaboration is designed to create mutual incentives for peace, as both nations stand to benefit more from cooperation than from prolonged conflict.

Additionally, the peace treaty includes provisions for equitable resource sharing, transparency, and joint oversight, ensuring that economic collaboration remains fair and sustainable. By emphasizing shared economic growth, *Project Lyubov* reframes the narrative of conflict into one of partnership, demonstrating that diplomacy and mutual prosperity can coexist.

Aligning Economic Policy with Peacebuilding Initiatives

Project Lyubov recognizes that sustainable peace requires more than diplomatic agreements—it requires economic policies that address the root causes of conflict, such as poverty, unemployment, and resource competition. By aligning economic policy with peacebuilding efforts, the initiative seeks to create conditions that promote stability and resilience.

One of the key aspects of this alignment is the reinvestment of marijuana revenues into community development programs in both Russia and Ukraine. These funds are directed toward education, healthcare, and public infrastructure projects that improve living conditions and create opportunities for growth. By providing tangible benefits to communities affected by conflict, the initiative fosters public support for peace efforts and demonstrates the practical value of cooperation.

Furthermore, *Project Lyubov* emphasizes the importance of international partnerships in maintaining peace. By involving IISF member nations as stakeholders and contributors, the initiative creates a network of allied countries committed to supporting peace through economic collaboration and scientific innovation. This collective effort reinforces the idea that peace is not solely the responsibility of the nations involved in the conflict but a shared global priority.

Mutual Prosperity Through International Cooperation

The ultimate goal of *Project Lyubov* is to build a framework for mutual prosperity that transcends political divides. By fostering economic interdependence, the initiative encourages Russia, Ukraine, and their allies to pursue shared goals, such as advancing space exploration, scientific research, and technological development. This shared prosperity model not only strengthens diplomatic ties but also positions participating nations as leaders in a global movement toward innovation and unity.

The program's focus on economic collaboration extends to space-related projects, with revenues supporting IISF-led initiatives aimed at planetary colonization, spacecraft development, and interstellar exploration. By contributing to these projects, Russia and Ukraine play active roles in shaping humanity's future in space, reinforcing their status as valuable partners in international progress.

Additionally, the program's emphasis on inclusive economic participation ensures that smaller communities and marginalized groups benefit from the peace-building efforts. By creating jobs, funding education, and improving healthcare, *Project Lyubov* addresses systemic inequalities and promotes social cohesion, making peace not only a diplomatic achievement but a foundation for long-term prosperity.

A Vision for Lasting Peace and Progress

Project Lyubov exemplifies how economic collaboration can serve as a bridge for peace, turning conflict zones into regions of opportunity and growth. By aligning economic policy with peacebuilding initiatives, the program demonstrates that diplomacy is most effective when it is supported by tangible investments in human development and community welfare.

Through mutual prosperity, international cooperation, and a shared commitment to innovation, *Project Lyubov* transforms the principles of peace into actionable strategies that benefit all stakeholders. The initiative stands as a testament to the belief that lasting peace is not achieved through division, but through unity, partnership, and a collective vision for a brighter future.

Chapter 12

Employment Opportunities and Professionalization

A critical pillar of *Project Walz* is its focus on employment creation and professionalization within the legal cannabis market. By building a robust industry that prioritizes inclusivity and skill development, the program creates pathways for individuals from all backgrounds—including those historically marginalized by drug policies—to enter legitimate, well-paying professions. This strategy not only fosters economic growth but also supports social reintegration, ensuring that individuals and communities most affected by prohibition can participate meaningfully in the industry's success.

Hiring and Training Qualified Personnel

The success of *Project Walz* depends on the recruitment and training of a highly skilled workforce capable of managing the complexities of the regulated cannabis market. This includes roles in cultivation, distribution, retail, compliance, and research. To meet this demand, the program invests in comprehensive training programs that equip individuals with the technical knowledge and professional skills needed to thrive in a legal industry.

These training initiatives are designed to be accessible, offering scholarships, mentorships, and on-the-job training opportunities for individuals from underserved communities, particularly foster care youth and former street-level dealers. The emphasis on professional development ensures that employees are not only knowledgeable about regulatory frameworks and safety protocols but are also empowered to pursue long-term careers in the industry.

By prioritizing workforce development, *Project Walz* positions the legal cannabis market as a dynamic and innovative sector that offers economic mobility and professional growth. This focus on education and training also strengthens public confidence in the industry by ensuring that all operations are managed by qualified and accountable professionals.

Collaborating with National Security Institutions

To ensure regulatory compliance and public safety, *Project Walz* collaborates closely with national security institutions such as the **CIA**, **FBI**, and **local law enforcement agencies**. These collaborations focus on developing robust security protocols, monitoring market activities, and addressing potential risks related to illegal diversion, fraud, and organized crime.

However, this collaboration goes beyond enforcement. The program integrates national security institutions into its workforce development strategy, leveraging their expertise to design training programs that emphasize safety, transparency, and accountability. Law enforcement agencies also play a key role in community engagement efforts, working alongside local leaders to build trust and promote cooperation between regulatory bodies and market participants.

By fostering partnerships with national security institutions, the program ensures that the legal cannabis market operates within a framework of integrity and oversight. This collaboration reinforces the program's commitment to maintaining public safety while supporting economic innovation.

Integrating Former Dealers as Entrepreneurs

A defining feature of *Project Walz* is its commitment to integrating former street-level dealers into the legal market as entrepreneurs and business owners. The program recognizes that these individuals possess valuable entrepreneurial skills, market knowledge, and customer networks that can be leveraged within a regulated framework. Rather than excluding these individuals, the initiative provides them with opportunities to transition into legitimate roles as stakeholders and partners.

Former dealers are offered support in the form of business training, legal resources, and access to ownership stakes in retail stores and corporations. Under the ownership model, local entrepreneurs—including former dealers—receive a five percent share in corporations and a fifty percent share in retail stores within their communities. This ownership structure not only incentivizes compliance but also empowers former dealers to build wealth, contribute to their local economies, and act as mentors for others seeking similar opportunities.

This approach serves as a model for economic reintegration, demonstrating how legalization can be a tool for social rehabilitation and economic empowerment. By transforming former dealers into legitimate business owners, the program reduces the illegal trade, promotes community development, and fosters a culture of accountability and entrepreneurship.

A Pathway to Economic Empowerment

By creating employment opportunities, fostering professionalization, and supporting entrepreneurship, *Project Walz* redefines what it means to build a legal cannabis industry. The program's emphasis on workforce development and economic inclusion ensures that individuals from all backgrounds have the chance to participate in and benefit from the industry's success.

Through strategic partnerships, comprehensive training programs, and inclusive ownership models, the initiative positions the legal market as a driver of economic mobility, social progress, and community resilience. *Project Walz* demonstrates that legalization is not simply a policy shift—it is an opportunity to build a more inclusive and prosperous future, one that empowers individuals to contribute to their communities and achieve their full potential.

CHAPTER 13

OVERCOMING SOCIAL AND POLITICAL RESISTANCE

T he path to legalizing marijuana and implementing *Project Walz* is not without challenges. Social and political resistance to legalization remains a significant obstacle, often fueled by deeply rooted concerns, misconceptions, and skepticism. For the program to succeed, it must address public fears, engage key stakeholders, and maintain transparency and accountability at every stage. By fostering trust and demonstrating the tangible benefits of legalization, *Project Walz* aims to shift the narrative from controversy to opportunity and progress.

Addressing Public Concerns and Misconceptions

One of the main barriers to widespread support for marijuana legalization is the persistence of outdated narratives. For decades, cannabis has been associated with addiction, crime, and social decay, perpetuated by anti-drug campaigns and punitive policies. These misconceptions have shaped public opinion, making some communities wary of legalization despite evidence to the contrary.

To overcome these concerns, *Project Walz* prioritizes public education initiatives that provide clear, science-based information about non-addictive marijuana and the safety measures built into the legal framework. The program highlights data from regions where legalization has led to reduced crime rates, increased tax revenue, and improved access to medical cannabis for patients with chronic conditions.

Educational campaigns also emphasize the program's safeguards, such as strict product regulation, real-time tracking systems, and limits on product strength and sales. By addressing concerns about safety, addiction, and youth exposure, these efforts help build public trust and dispel myths that have long surrounded marijuana use.

Engaging Stakeholders for Support

Legalization efforts require collaboration and buy-in from a diverse range of stakeholders, including government officials, community leaders, law enforcement agencies, healthcare providers, and private sector partners. To build a coalition of support, *Project Walz* implements a multi-level engagement strategy designed to foster dialogue, build consensus, and address stakeholder concerns.

At the community level, town halls, workshops, and public forums are held to facilitate open discussions about the goals and benefits of legalization. Community members are encouraged to voice their questions and concerns, ensuring that local perspectives are integrated into the program's implementation.

At the institutional level, *Project Walz* partners with educational organizations, healthcare institutions, and law enforcement agencies to align the program's objectives with broader public interests. By involving these stakeholders in the design and oversight of the legal market, the initiative demonstrates its commitment to collaboration and shared responsibility.

Additionally, international allies within the **International Intergalactic Space Federation (IISF)** are engaged as economic partners, strengthening diplomatic relations and reinforcing the program's global vision. By framing legalization as a tool for economic development and international cooperation, the initiative garners support from both domestic and global stakeholders.

Ensuring Transparency and Accountability

Transparency and accountability are fundamental to maintaining public trust and ensuring the long-term success of *Project Walz*. The program includes several measures designed to promote openness and hold all participants accountable for their roles in the legal cannabis market.

First, the program mandates the use of publicly accessible reporting systems that track sales, tax revenues, and fund allocations. This ensures that the public can see how marijuana-related revenues are being reinvested into education, healthcare, and community development. Regular audits and reports further reinforce the program's commitment to transparency and fiscal responsibility.

Second, compliance mechanisms are built into every stage of the supply chain. Licensing requirements, real-time tracking, and independent oversight bodies are implemented to monitor operations and address potential violations. These measures not only prevent fraud and illegal activity but also ensure that corporations, retailers, and government agencies adhere to the program's ethical and legal standards.

Finally, *Project Walz* promotes accountability by fostering a culture of inclusion and representation. Community advisory boards, composed of local leaders, educators, and advocates, are established to provide ongoing feedback and recommendations. These boards help ensure that the program remains responsive to community needs and maintains its focus on social equity and justice.

A Blueprint for Change

Overcoming social and political resistance requires more than policy changes—it requires a commitment to transparency, collaboration, and education. By addressing misconceptions, engaging stakeholders, and demonstrating accountability, *Project Walz* sets a new standard for how legalization initiatives can foster public trust and drive meaningful reform.

Through its emphasis on dialogue, shared responsibility, and public engagement, the program positions itself as a catalyst for change, transforming legalization from a contentious issue into a unifying strategy for economic growth, social progress, and international cooperation.

CHAPTER 14

A VISION FOR AN INCLUSIVE FUTURE

The legalization initiative outlined in *Project Walz* represents much more than an economic reform—it embodies a vision for an inclusive and prosperous future. By leveraging legalization as a tool for societal progress, the program seeks to address systemic inequalities, empower marginalized communities, and foster economic resilience. The broader implications of this initiative extend beyond individual states and nations, positioning legalization as a global movement toward unity, innovation, and exploration.

The Broader Implications of Legalization

At its core, *Project Walz* demonstrates how thoughtful policy reform can create ripple effects that extend across multiple sectors. By formalizing the cannabis market and reinvesting revenues into public goods, the program addresses historical injustices perpetuated by prohibition while providing new pathways for economic participation.

Legalization is reframed not as a concession, but as an opportunity to cultivate thriving local economies, reduce incarceration rates, and support international collaboration through the **International Intergalactic Space Federation (IISF)**. This initiative challenges traditional narratives, illustrating how an industry long associated with criminalization can be transformed into a cornerstone of public welfare, scientific advancement, and economic development.

Investing in Youth and Community Prosperity

One of the program's most significant contributions is its commitment to education and healthcare, particularly for foster care children and underserved communities. By funding initiatives such as the **Garbuz Space School Academies**, *Project Walz* invests in the next generation of leaders, scientists, and innovators. These academies provide talented youth with the tools they need to pursue meaningful careers, not only in the legal cannabis market but also in emerging fields such as space exploration, biotechnology, and engineering.

This focus on education is complemented by investments in healthcare programs that ensure every individual has access to preventive care, mental health services, and specialized treatment. By addressing the root causes of poverty and inequality, the program strengthens communities and fosters social cohesion. Families that once struggled with limited resources can now benefit from free, high-quality services that improve their quality of life and expand their opportunities for success.

Community prosperity is further supported through job creation, entrepreneurship programs, and reintegration initiatives for former street-level dealers. By providing legitimate economic opportunities, the program transforms individuals from marginalized backgrounds into active contributors to their local economies, breaking cycles of poverty and fostering long-term stability.

Building a World of Unity, Progress, and Exploration

Beyond its economic and social impacts, *Project Walz* positions legalization as a foundation for global unity and scientific progress. By reinvesting revenues into IISF-led space exploration projects, the program advances humanity's collective dream of expanding its presence beyond Earth. This reinvestment underscores the belief that technological innovation and interplanetary exploration are not luxuries but shared global priorities that require collaboration, creativity, and resource-sharing.

The partnerships fostered through this initiative create a global network of nations united by a common purpose—to explore new frontiers, discover sustainable solutions for life in space, and push the boundaries of human potential. This vision transcends political divides, demonstrating that economic reform can serve as a bridge for peace, unity, and progress.

By aligning economic policy with scientific ambition and humanitarian values, *Project Walz* illustrates how legalization can create a more interconnected and inclusive world. The program's commitment to shared prosperity and international cooperation lays the groundwork for a future defined not by competition, but by collaboration and discovery.

A Call to Action

Project Walz invites policymakers, communities, and individuals to imagine what is possible when bold ideas are paired with purposeful action. By investing in youth, fostering economic inclusion, and prioritizing public welfare, the program sets a precedent for how legalization can be a catalyst for positive change.

The vision presented here is not just about reform—it is about transformation. It is a vision of a world where every individual, regardless of their background, has the opportunity to thrive. It is a vision of global alliances built on trust and mutual benefit, and of a humanity united in its pursuit of knowledge, progress, and exploration.

By embracing this vision, we take a step toward building a brighter future—one where innovation, equity, and opportunity are not aspirations but realities for all.

AFTERWORD

Dear Readers,

At the heart of *Project Walz* lies a bold vision—one where economic reform serves as a pathway to equity, opportunity, and global progress. This book explores how legalization, when approached with purpose and responsibility, can be a catalyst for social transformation, empowering communities, fostering unity, and funding humanity's greatest endeavors.

Through these pages, we've examined a future where revenues from legalization create free education, universal healthcare, and career pathways for those who have long been left behind. This book is not just an account of an ambitious initiative—it is a call to action. Every effort toward making this vision a reality helps build a more inclusive world where prosperity and innovation are within everyone's reach.

By supporting this initiative, you are joining a movement that turns former cycles of inequality into opportunities for empowerment. You are contributing to the establishment of businesses that uplift communities, programs that transform foster care education, and partnerships that unite nations in the shared goal of scientific exploration and interplanetary discovery.

This project is about more than economic reform; it is about building a future where collaboration triumphs over division, where every person has the chance to rise, and where humanity's next chapter in space exploration is written together.

Thank you for being part of this journey. Your belief in this vision fuels progress and brings us closer to a world of shared dreams and limitless horizons. Together, we can build not just a better tomorrow but a future that inspires generations to come.

Proudly sponsored by GarbuzSpace.com

Za Detey – For Kids!

Za Lyubov – For Love!

Live, Make, & Enjoy!